is a gift... don't trash it!

53 Things
Everyone Should Know

John W. Alston

LIFE IS A GIFT...DON'T TRASH IT
53 Things Everyone Should Know

John W. Alston

ISBN 1-890630-00-4

Published by John Alston presents...
419 N. Larchmont Blvd., No. 9, Los Angeles, CA 90004
(800) 200-9225

Printed in the United States of America

Desktop Publishing
Jeff Crume, Upward Bound Productions

Acknowledgments

Many people have enriched my life, uplifted my spirit, and helped me make this simple tome possible. A special thanks, however, is due to my patient wife, Karen and my daughter, Lindsay.

A particular thanks goes to Micky Fisher for being there for me through thick and thin. And last but not least, Jeff Crume. Jeff you are a special friend and colleague, who sat down with me as we opened our veins to simplify and bring to paper what I so easily state from the platform. Words are not enough to say thanks, but on paper it is all I have. So again, I say thank you for being there and for being who you are.

Dedication

To all of those striving to
heal the world, accept human nature
and make peace with reality.

Introduction

It is no accident that you picked up this book! You were either in attendance at one of my presentations or intrigued by the title as you saw the book on display. In either case, you are fortunate.

This book presents fifty-three ideas for you to ponder and apply to your daily life. One new idea for each week of the year. The remaining idea is presented as idea #1. Affirm it daily with each subsequent idea. Commit each of these ideas to memory, and at the end of the year you will have learned fifty-three things that will impact your life forever!

Review each idea daily. The challenge here is to re-train your mind in order to get a hold of your behavior. After reviewing each "idea of the week," respond to it's significance by answering the following questions: *What's the point? How does knowing this change anything? What am I going to do now?*

This is work, but recommending that you do less reduces this book to just another collection of quaint sayings. The choice is yours. If you want more out of your life, you need to do what is necessary. The best antidote for failure, depression, despair and mental frustration is to take action! **What are you waiting for?**

Think...When was the last time you learned anything that caused you to change your behavior for the better?

A Word from John Alston

This book will help you shape a perspective about life. It does not offer any specific *"all you gotta do's."* It is simply designed to stimulate your thinking and provide ideas that can help change your life for the better. Use it, and it will serve you well...Guaranteed!

There are many things we are required to know in order to live well. The problem is, we come into life without instructions. Our development is basically left up to significant others. They either pass on to us the knowledge we need to succeed in life, or they don't. Without the assistance of others, we are left to fend on our own.

Growing up, I was exposed to ideas that stressed the importance of status, glamour, material things, and being rich. Believing that these things were essential to living well, I worked hard at acquiring them. I sold products door to door, bussed tables, parked cars, and sold clothes. I was a bell hop, veterinarian assistant, theme park attendant, and director of an institute. I was a counselor, school teacher, educational consultant, and now a professional speaker.

Looking back, I realize that these jobs made it possible for me to acquire things, however, more importantly, they helped me shape a new perspective about living well. This new perspective led to discover my life's ultimate work...helping people.

A Word from John Alston

I have learned that while money does make for independence, certain ways of living are more fulfilling than others. I now understand that living well has more to do with maturing, achieving inner stability, and developing character, decency and common sense.

It is now my goal to pass on to you those same ideas and insight that I have collected over the years. In this book you will find 53 ideas that, if put into practice, can make the same impact on your life as they have on mine. I know this is easy to say and hard to do, but what isn't? You need only be willing to do the work by reading one idea per week and acting on it. This is the ultimate "balm for the soul," **so start now!**

1

Life is a gift...Don't trash it.
Everything you have, experience, or
acquire is a gift that enables you
to grow and live well.

**53
Things**

What's the point?

_____

_____

_____

How does knowing this change anything?

_____

_____

_____

What am I going to do now?

_____

_____

_____

2

*O*nce you are conscious of life's
gifts, you are responsible.
Nothing gets you off the hook!

**53
Things**

Everyone Should Know

What's the point?

_____

_____

_____

How does knowing this change anything?

_____

_____

_____

What am I going to do now?

_____

_____

_____

**53
Things**
Everyone Should Know

3

The greatest gift you have is your mind...Develop it!

53
Things

Everyone Should Know

What's the point?

_____

_____

_____

How does knowing this change anything?

_____

_____

_____

What am I going to do now?

_____

_____

_____

**53
Things**

4

If you don't control your
mind, someone else will.
All it takes is a good story.

**53
Things**

What's the point?

_____

_____

_____

How does knowing this change anything?

_____

_____

_____

What am I going to do now?

_____

_____

_____

**53
Things**

Everyone Should Know

5

A lie is as powerful as the truth if you can get someone to believe it.

53 Things

Everyone Should Know

What's the point?

_____

_____

_____

How does knowing this change anything?

_____

_____

_____

What am I going to do now?

_____

_____

_____

**53
Things**

6

You have freedom of choice,
but never freedom from
consequence.

53
Things

What's the point?

_____

_____

_____

How does knowing this change anything?

_____

_____

_____

What am I going to do now?

_____

_____

_____

**53
Things**

7

Decency Counts. Be as decent a human being as you can be...

*When things are broken...
get with others and fix them.*

~

*When things are dirty...
clean them up.*

~

*When there is an injustice...
make things right.*

~

*When you see someone suffering...
reach out to help them.*

53 Things

Everyone Should Know

What's the point?

_____

_____

_____

How does knowing this change anything?

_____

_____

_____

What am I going to do now?

_____

_____

_____

53
Things
Everyone Should Know

8

Problems in life never go away...
Get better at handling them
or they will handle you.

What's the point?

_____

_____

_____

How does knowing this change anything?

_____

_____

_____

What am I going to do now?

_____

_____

_____

53
Things

9

We all have privileges, strengths and abilities... Take advantage of yours.

Remember: There is no guarantee on time...Begin now!

53 Things

What's the point?

_____

_____

_____

How does knowing this change anything?

_____

_____

_____

What am I going to do now?

_____

_____

_____

10

There are two kinds of
situations in life:
Controllable & Uncontrollable.

If it's controllable...Act on it!
If it is uncontrollable...Change your
attitude toward it!

**53
Things**

What's the point?

_____

_____

_____

How does knowing this change anything?

_____

_____

_____

What am I going to do now?

_____

_____

_____

53
Things

11

The belief in the permanence of
a controllable situation
robs the believer of the ability
to change the situation.

**53
Things**

Everyone Should Know

What's the point?

_____

_____

_____

How does knowing this change anything?

_____

_____

_____

What am I going to do now?

_____

_____

_____

**53
Things**

Everyone Should Know

12

It does no good to complain
to someone who doesn't
care or can't help.

What's the point?

_____

_____

_____

How does knowing this change anything?

_____

_____

_____

What am I going to do now?

_____

_____

_____

53
Things
Everyone Should Know

13

Boredom emerges from
lack of purpose...Get clear
on why you are here!

What's the point?

_____

_____

_____

How does knowing this change anything?

_____

_____

_____

What am I going to do now?

_____

_____

_____

**53
Things**

14

Life, in many ways, is like a game.
There are rules, boundaries,
time limits, contingencies, and
most important...goals.
Knowing the goal is essential.

**53
Things**

What's the point?

_____

_____

_____

How does knowing this change anything?

_____

_____

_____

What am I going to do now?

_____

_____

_____

15

The goal in the game of life is to develop your talents and skills and then give them back to the world.

What's the point?

_____

_____

_____

How does knowing this change anything?

_____

_____

_____

What am I going to do now?

_____

_____

_____

**53
Things**

Everyone Should Know

16

You are born and you die...
everything in between
is negotiable.

53
Things

What's the point?

_____

_____

_____

How does knowing this change anything?

_____

_____

_____

What am I going to do now?

_____

_____

_____

17

If you woke up today,
you are in the game...You
have another shot at it.

**53
Things**

What's the point?

_____

_____

_____

How does knowing this change anything?

_____

_____

_____

What am I going to do now?

_____

_____

_____

53
Things

18

All human achievement begins
with the idea that it is possible.
In order for dreams to come true
you must first wake up!

**53
Things**

Everyone Should Know

What's the point?

_____

_____

_____

How does knowing this change anything?

_____

_____

_____

What am I going to do now?

_____

_____

_____

**53
Things**

19

*G*oals do not guarantee
success...They merely increase
your chances of success.

**53
Things**

What's the point?

_____

_____

_____

How does knowing this change anything?

_____

_____

_____

What am I going to do now?

_____

_____

_____

53
Things

20

Visions become goals...Goals
deserves plans...Plans require
strategies, effort and
corrective action.

Evaluation is the attention
given to action.

**53
Things**

What's the point?

_____

_____

_____

How does knowing this change anything?

_____

_____

_____

What am I going to do now?

_____

_____

_____

21

No matter what happens, good, bad, bitter or sweet, nothing lasts forever...Still life goes on.

What's the point?

_____

_____

_____

How does knowing this change anything?

_____

_____

_____

What am I going to do now?

_____

_____

_____

22

The only difference between
salad and garbage is
time and arrangement.

**53
Things**

What's the point?

_____

_____

_____

How does knowing this change anything?

_____

_____

_____

What am I going to do now?

_____

_____

_____

23

You can get anything you want as a result of how you present yourself.

53 Things

Everyone Should Know

What's the point?

_____

_____

_____

How does knowing this change anything?

_____

_____

_____

What am I going to do now?

_____

_____

_____

53
Things

24

No one will *do* for you that which you must *do* for yourself.

53
Things

What's the point?

_____

_____

_____

How does knowing this change anything?

_____

_____

_____

What am I going to do now?

_____

_____

_____

It's true, if it's going to be, it's up to me; at the same time realize no one ever achieves anything alone.

53 Things

Everyone Should Know

What's the point?

_____

_____

_____

How does knowing this change anything?

_____

_____

_____

What am I going to do now?

_____

_____

_____

**53
Things**

26

Prejudice denies access to the
support, talent and ability
that those you prejudge
might bring to you.

**53
Things**

Everyone Should Know

What's the point?

_____

_____

_____

How does knowing this change anything?

_____

_____

_____

What am I going to do now?

_____

_____

_____

53
Things

27

People tend to believe what they want in spite of what the facts may be.

53 Things

What's the point?

_____

_____

_____

How does knowing this change anything?

_____

_____

_____

What am I going to do now?

_____

_____

_____

53 Things

28

People tend to reject and react negatively to things they don't understand.

53 Things

Everyone Should Know

What's the point?

_____

_____

_____

How does knowing this change anything?

_____

_____

_____

What am I going to do now?

_____

_____

_____

29

Maturity is a matter of being able to impose discipline over your impulses, and being aware of how your behavior affects others.

53 Things

Everyone Should Know

What's the point?

_____

_____

_____

How does knowing this change anything?

_____

_____

_____

What am I going to do now?

_____

_____

_____

**53
Things**

30

The life you live affirms the conduct you endorse.

Remember: Your integrity is easier to retain than to recover.

53 Things

What's the point?

_____

_____

_____

How does knowing this change anything?

_____

_____

_____

What am I going to do now?

_____

_____

_____

31

Be tolerant of those who
are less informed than you.

Remember: You can't uplift
others by humiliating them!

**53
Things**

What's the point?

_____

_____

_____

How does knowing this change anything?

_____

_____

_____

What am I going to do now?

_____

_____

_____

32

Surround yourself with
good people...Chances are that if
you lay down with dogs you
are destined to get up
with some fleas.

**53
Things**

What's the point?

_____

_____

_____

How does knowing this change anything?

_____

_____

_____

What am I going to do now?

_____

_____

_____

**53
Things**
Everyone Should Know

33

You will not please everyone,
nor will you be loved by everyone.

If Moses, Jesus, Mohammed,
Socrates, Buddha, or Confucius
did not win 100% of the people...
Who do you think you are?

**53
Things**

What's the point?

_____

_____

_____

How does knowing this change anything?

_____

_____

_____

What am I going to do now?

_____

_____

_____

**53
Things**

34

There is only one race of people on the planet...The human race.

Amongst them there are two groups: The decent and indecent. You may choose the one to which you want to belong.

53 Things

Everyone Should Know

What's the point?

_____

_____

_____

How does knowing this change anything?

_____

_____

_____

What am I going to do now?

_____

_____

_____

35

It's always easier to get into a situation than it is to get out of one.

You can't talk yourself out of something that you behaved yourself into.

**53
Things**

Everyone Should Know

What's the point?

_____

_____

_____

How does knowing this change anything?

_____

_____

_____

What am I going to do now?

_____

_____

_____

It's not what happens to you
that counts as much as how you
respond to what happens.

**53
Things**

What's the point?

_____

_____

_____

How does knowing this change anything?

_____

_____

_____

What am I going to do now?

_____

_____

_____

37

We all need reminders of the
things we already know.

What's the point?

_____

_____

_____

How does knowing this change anything?

_____

_____

_____

What am I going to do now?

_____

_____

_____

53
Things
Everyone Should Know

38

Just because you know better
doesn't mean you're going
to do better.

53
Things
Everyone Should Know

What's the point?

_____

_____

_____

How does knowing this change anything?

_____

_____

_____

What am I going to do now?

_____

_____

_____

**53
Things**

39

There is never a single explanation
for human faults or failings...
Only reasons or excuses.

**53
Things**

What's the point?

_____

_____

_____

How does knowing this change anything?

_____

_____

_____

What am I going to do now?

_____

_____

_____

**53
Things**

40

The one thing that we can
predict about people is
that they are unpredictable.

What's the point?

_____

_____

_____

How does knowing this change anything?

_____

_____

_____

What am I going to do now?

_____

_____

_____

**53
Things**

41

*P*eople tend to see that which they are looking with.

*O*ptimists see opportunity, pessimists see none.

**53
Things**

What's the point?

_____

_____

_____

How does knowing this change anything?

_____

_____

_____

What am I going to do now?

_____

_____

_____

53
Things
Everyone Should Know

42

For every negative observation you make, find a noteworthy positive one somewhere else.

What's the point?

_____

_____

_____

How does knowing this change anything?

_____

_____

_____

What am I going to do now?

_____

_____

_____

53
Things

43

Frustration is an essential
part of life. Nothing is created
or changed without first
becoming frustrated.

Never confuse what is hard to do
with what is impossible to do.

**53
Things**

What's the point?

_____

_____

_____

How does knowing this change anything?

_____

_____

_____

What am I going to do now?

_____

_____

_____

44

Pain is nature's way of
getting your attention.

Pain is inevitable...
Suffering is optional.

What's the point?

_____

_____

_____

How does knowing this change anything?

_____

_____

_____

What am I going to do now?

_____

_____

_____

45

Feelings never tell us what to do, they only alert us to the things that require our attention.

Remember: Not feeling like doing the right thing is no excuse for not doing the right thing.

**53
Things**

What's the point?

_____

_____

_____

How does knowing this change anything?

_____

_____

_____

What am I going to do now?

_____

_____

_____

53
Things

46

Make it 100% ok to receive criticism.

**53
Things**

What's the point?

_____

_____

_____

How does knowing this change anything?

_____

_____

_____

What am I going to do now?

_____

_____

_____

53
Things

47

Your weaknesses always lead
you to that which you
are supposed to learn.

**53
Things**

What's the point?

_____

_____

_____

How does knowing this change anything?

_____

_____

_____

What am I going to do now?

_____

_____

_____

Worrying never prevents a
mistake or provides a solution
unless it motivates us
to take action.

53
Things

What's the point?

_____

_____

_____

How does knowing this change anything?

_____

_____

_____

What am I going to do now?

_____

_____

_____

49

In order to be free, you must first be a slave...A slave to discipline.

**53
Things**

What's the point?

_____

_____

_____

How does knowing this change anything?

_____

_____

_____

What am I going to do now?

_____

_____

_____

**53
Things**

50

Y̶ou cannot hold on to faith and
fear at the same time.

**53
Things**

Everyone Should Know

What's the point?

_____

_____

_____

How does knowing this change anything?

_____

_____

_____

What am I going to do now?

_____

_____

_____

**53
Things**
Everyone Should Know

51

*G*ratitude is essential to living well!   Ask "Why me" when good things happen as well as bad.

53
Things

Everyone Should Know

What's the point?

_____

_____

_____

How does knowing this change anything?

_____

_____

_____

What am I going to do now?

_____

_____

_____

53
Things

52

Living well *does not prevent*
failure or *disappointment*...
It merely assists in
achieving balance.

**53
Things**

What's the point?

_____

_____

_____

How does knowing this change anything?

_____

_____

_____

What am I going to do now?

_____

_____

_____

*G*ratitude is a positive attitude
that influences behavior.
Choose your attitude, and
remember that no achievements
have ever been attained without
a positive attitude!

**53
Things**

What's the point?

_____

_____

_____

How does knowing this change anything?

_____

_____

_____

What am I going to do now?

_____

_____

_____

**53
Things**

A Final Note On Common Sense

If you have ever been dismayed or surprised at someone's lapse in judgement or outright stupidity, you may have asked, *"Why didn't they just use common sense?"* You would think they would know better. What is common sense anyway? Common sense is basic knowledge we assume to be commonly held by everyone. It includes observations and strategies, that when forgotten or ignored, compel us to ask, *"What the *#@&! were they thinking?"*

From time to time, even the most educated people make *boneheaded* decisions reflecting in a lapse in judgement. No matter who it is, when one acts naively, senselessly, recklessly, immorally or lawlessly, we will always ask, *"What the *#@&! were you thinking?"*

If you know of someone who needs a good dose of common sense, order this book for them today!

If you have a definition of common sense or any additional *things* you think everyone should know, I'd like to hear from you. I'm interested in news clippings, stories, or any examples you find that would qualify as a "boneheaded" decision, or violate common sense. Please send your findings and comments to: **John Alston presents... 419 N. Larchmont Bl., No. 9, Los Angeles, CA 90004**, or fax them to me at **(213) 857-6626.**

Remember...

Your Life Is A Gift...Don't Trash It!

For More Information:

John Alston presents...
419 N. Larchmont Bl., No. 9
Los Angeles, CA 90004
Phone (800) 200-9225
Fax (213) 857-6626
email: windjohn@aol.com
http://www.expertcenter.com/members/jwals3/